GETTING TO KNOW
THE U.S. PRESIDENTS

# THEODORE
# ROOSEVELT

TWENTY-SIXTH PRESIDENT
1901 – 1909

WRITTEN AND ILLUSTRATED BY MIKE VENEZIA

D0125475

CHILDREN'S PRESS®
A DIVISION OF SCHOLASTIC INC.
NEW YORK   TORONTO   LONDON   AUCKLAND   SYDNEY
MEXICO CITY   NEW DELHI   HONG KONG
DANBURY, CONNECTICUT

Reading Consultant: Nanci R. Vargus, Ed.D., Assistant Professor, School of Education, University of Indianapolis

Historical Consultant: Marc J. Selverstone, Ph.D., Assistant Professor, Miller Center of Public Affairs, University of Virginia

Photographs © 2007: Corbis Images: 8, 32 (Bettmann), 15 top left (Farrell Grehan), 15 top right (Steve Kaufman), 28 (Pat O'Hara), 11, 29; Frederic Remington Art Museum, Ogdensburg, New York: 22 (Charge of the Rough Riders, by Frederic Remington, 1898, oil on canvas, 35 x 60 in.); Getty Images/Amy Taborsky: 15 bottom; Library of Congress: 19 (George Yost Coffin), 27 (Udo J. Keppler), 16 bottom, 17, 18, 23; The Art Archive/Picture Desk: 30 (Louis Dalrymple/Culver Pictures), 14; Theodore Roosevelt Collection, Harvard College Library: 6 (via SODA), 10, 13, 20, 26; White House Historical Association/White House Collection: 3 (Image# 56).

Colorist for illustrations: Dave Ludwig

Library of Congress Cataloging-in-Publication Data

Venezia, Mike.
  Theodore Roosevelt / written and illustrated by Mike Venezia.
    p. cm. — (Getting to know the U.S. presidents)
  ISBN 10: 0-516-22630-4 (lib. bdg.)   0-516-25225-9 (pbk.)
  ISBN 13: 978-0-516-22630-9 (lib. bdg.)   978-0-516-25225-4 (pbk.)
  1. Roosevelt, Theodore, 1858-1919—Juvenile literature. 2. Presidents—United States—Biography—Juvenile literature. I. Title.
  E757.V46 2006
  973.91'1092-dc22

                                                    2006000459

1 2 3 4 5 6 7 8 9 10 R 16 15 14 13 12 11 10 09 08 07

A portrait of President Theodore Roosevelt by John Singer Sargent

T heodore Roosevelt was the twenty-sixth president of the United States. He was born into a wealthy New York family on October 27, 1858. Theodore grew up to be a remarkable man. Before he became president, he studied to be a naturalist, learned to box, was a real cowboy out West, wrote some important books, and became a war hero!

Theodore Roosevelt was probably the most energetic president the United States ever had. Some people described him as having flames coming out of his ears! As president, Teddy worked hard to control large greedy businesses. He pushed forward the building of the Panama Canal. He set aside millions or acres of land for national forests, parks, and wildlife refuges. President Roosevelt even won the Nobel Peace Prize for helping end a war between Japan and Russia.

After Teddy finished being president, he went on a year-long African safari. He later explored a dangerous, uncharted river in South America. Teddy collected thousands of animal trophies and nature samples for American museums. If someone were to choose a president to make into a super-action-hero figure, it would have to be Teddy Roosevelt.

"Teedie" Roosevelt at age four

Even though Teddy Roosevelt was a high-powered, active adult, he didn't start out that way. Teddy, or Teedie, as his family called him, was a sickly boy. He had bad asthma, stomach problems, and terrible eyesight. Teedie was too thin and weak to go to school, so he was taught at home. He was very smart and loved to read, especially heroic tales and adventure books.

Teedie also loved studying animals and birds. He collected animal skulls and bones, mice, frogs, turtles, snakes, and bugs. He put together his own "museum of natural history." Teedie made scientific notes and drawings of his collection. Sometimes visitors were shocked by the collection, but Mr. and Mrs. Roosevelt always encouraged their son.

In the late 1800s, the wealthy Roosevelt family gave money and time to help poor New York city families like this one.

The Roosevelts were a very generous family. They shared their wealth and much of their time helping the poor people of New York City. Mr. and Mrs. Roosevelt also took time to educate their children. Twice while Teedie was growing up, his parents took him and his brother and sisters on year-long trips to Europe, Egypt, and other foreign places.

Teedie was becoming well educated, but his body was still in pretty bad shape. Finally, his father challenged him to make his body strong. Teedie accepted the challenge. He began a serious workout program that included exercises, weightlifting, and boxing. After months of hard work, Teddy Roosevelt made his weak, scrawny body into one of a powerful athlete.

When he was eighteen years old, Teddy entered Harvard College. He hoped to become a naturalist, a scientist who studies animals and plants. Sadly, Teddy's father died during his son's second year at college.

A few months later, a happier event occurred. Teddy met a girl named Alice Lee. Teddy and Alice ended up falling in love and getting married.

By the time he reached Harvard, Theodore Roosevelt had become quite athletic. Here he is shown posing in his college rowing outfit.

Alice Hathaway Lee Roosevelt in the early 1880s

Teddy soon changed his mind about his career. He realized naturalists didn't make much money. He knew he would have to make another career choice if he wanted to someday support a family. Teddy decided to join a political group called the Republican Party. He had a feeling he would be good at watching out for people's rights and helping run the government.

Republican Party members quickly noticed Teddy Roosevelt. They saw an energetic young man who had intelligent opinions on just about everything. They soon asked Teddy to run for political office. Teddy ran for the position of New York State assemblyman and won.

Theodore Roosevelt won his first election in 1881, at the age of twenty-three. Right from the beginning, he surprised people. He always spoke up and did what he thought was right to protect and help the citizens of New York. Teddy did this even if it meant going against the wishes of the most powerful members of his political party.

Theodore Roosevelt (standing, right) with fellow New York State assemblymen

Everything seemed to be going great for Teddy. Then, in 1884, a terrible tragedy happened. Soon after giving birth to the Roosevelts' first baby, Alice became very ill and died. To make matters even worse, on that very same day in the same house, Teddy's mother also died. Teddy managed to finish up some of his duties, but he was too sad and upset to continue with his job.

Roosevelt in 1885, when he was living on his ranch in the Dakotas

Teddy asked his sister to watch his new baby daughter, Alice, for a while. He then took off for the Wild West. Some years earlier, Teddy had bought a ranch in the Badlands of the Dakota Territory. He decided to spend time there, raising cattle, being a cowboy, and dealing with the loss of his wife and mother.

Theodore Roosevelt escaped from his grief by retreating to this cabin (above and right) in the Dakota Territory (below).

Roosevelt in a hunting suit in 1885

At first, cowboys and ranchers in the area made fun of Roosevelt. Teddy dressed the way he thought a cowboy should look, and he spoke in an educated, formal way that no one in the West was used to. It didn't take long, though, before Teddy won the respect of local cowboys.

Roosevelt with his horse in the Dakotas

Teddy worked alongside wranglers, roping and branding cattle. He loved doing all the other ranch jobs, too. Teddy even became a deputy sheriff and once captured a gang of outlaws! After spending two years on the range, Teddy returned to New York City to take care of little Alice and get involved in politics again.

Just before Teddy Roosevelt began working on his political career, he ran into an old childhood friend, Edith Carow. Teddy and Edith had always liked each other while they were growing up. They soon started dating, got engaged, and got married. Teddy and Edith would end up having five children.

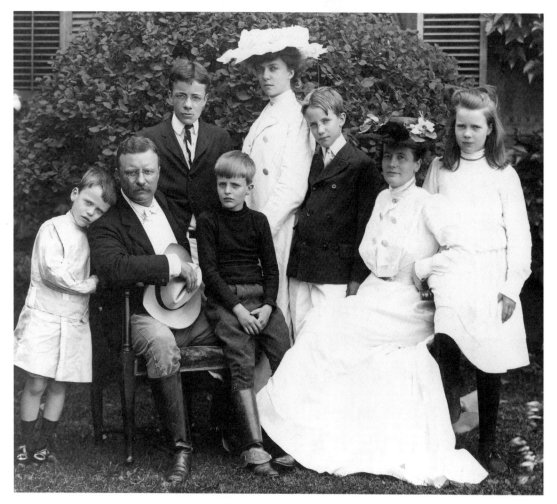

Theodore Roosevelt with his family in the early 1900s

This political cartoon, titled "A Roosevelt to the Rescue," shows Roosevelt as a tough New York City police commissioner.

Republican Party members were now anxious to help Teddy get elected or appointed to all kinds of important jobs. One of those jobs was New York City police commissioner. When Teddy found out there were loads of crooked, lazy policemen in the department, he started firing them right away. Teddy couldn't stand dishonest policemen. He even fired the city's corrupt chief of police!

Colonel Theodore Roosevelt (standing in center) and the Rough Riders

In 1897, Teddy got a new job when President William McKinley appointed him assistant secretary of the Navy. In 1898, the Spanish-American War began. Teddy was all for the war, and surprised people by leaving his important job to join the army. He helped form a special group of fighters that became known as the Rough Riders. As soon as they were trained, Lieutenant Colonel Roosevelt and his men left for the island of Cuba, where part of the war was being fought.

Many of the Rough Riders were handpicked by Teddy, who wanted only the best riflemen and horsemen. It was an unusual group, made up of cowboys, prospectors, and Native Americans. Teddy even asked some brainy athletes and well-mannered gentlemen from Harvard to join up. Teddy Roosevelt fearlessly led the Rough Riders into battle.

*The Charge of the Rough Riders,* by Frederic Remington (Frederic Remington Art Museum, Ogdensburg, NY)

When the war ended, about 100 days after it began, the United States had won. Teddy was proud of his country. He saw the Spanish-American War as a way of freeing the Cuban people from their cruel Spanish rulers. Teddy often felt the United States should help poor, weak nations, whether those nations wanted help or not.

Teddy Roosevelt returned to New York a national hero. Soon he was asked to run for governor of New York State. Republican Party members helped Teddy campaign, and thanks to their help, he won the election.

A campaign poster from the 1898 race for governor of New York State

As governor of New York, Theodore Roosevelt continued to do things his way. He ignored requests from party members if he felt the requests were dishonest or unfair. Since Governor Roosevelt wasn't cooperating with the Republican Party bosses, they soon wanted to get rid of him, but they didn't know how to do it.

Then, an unexpected event happened that changed everything. The vice president of the United States died. President William McKinley needed a replacement right away. Teddy's party bosses thought if they could convince Teddy to run for vice president in the next election, they could get Teddy out of their hair forever.

President William McKinley (left) and Theodore Roosevelt (right)

Teddy Roosevelt accepted the offer. He ran for and was elected President McKinley's vice president in 1901.

Soon another event happened that would change the history of the United States. On September 6, 1901, President McKinley was shot and killed by a mentally disturbed man. Suddenly, at age forty-three, Theodore Roosevelt became the youngest president of the United States.

TR, as he was often called at the time, was made for the job of president. He loved it! TR went to work right away. He helped get laws passed that would make things better for average working people. President Roosevelt urged the Justice Department to bring lawsuits against large, greedy companies that controlled prices to keep them high. He also pushed for laws to stop companies from packaging and selling unsafe food and drugs.

This 1904 political cartoon shows President Roosevelt getting ready to fight the "giants" of big business.

President Roosevelt made conservation a big part of his presidency. Even in the early 1900s, he could see that it would be easy for the nation's forests to be used up someday. He was afraid that houses and buildings would destroy beautiful scenic areas, too. President Roosevelt preserved millions of acres of magnificent wilderness areas forever.

President Roosevelt worked to make sure that such natural treasures as the Grand Canyon would be preserved forever.

The building of the Panama Canal was one of Teddy Roosevelt's major projects.

TR was also proud to have started the U.S. project to build the Panama Canal. The canal was a shortcut between the Atlantic and Pacific Oceans. When it was finally completed in 1914, it allowed navy ships, as well as other ships, to travel between oceans in days instead of months.

THE WORLD'S CONSTABLE.

A political cartoon showing President Roosevelt with a "big stick"

When it came to dealing with foreign countries, TR's favorite saying was "Speak softly and carry a big stick." This meant the United States would be willing to talk problems out with other nations, but would always be ready to use force if necessary.

TR wasn't the only one who loved his job as president. His family enjoyed it right along

with him. All six of the Roosevelt children had free run of the White House. There were bicycles and toys all over the front lawn. Sometimes the children brought their pet pony inside. Snakes and mice were other favorite pets. The Roosevelt kids were even known to drop water balloons on the heads of White House guards!

Even after his presidency, Theodore Roosevelt continued to make public speeches about important issues.

President Roosevelt left the White House after his second term ended in 1909. He kept busy, taking adventure trips, writing books, hunting, and fishing. TR even ran for president again in 1912, but he didn't win.

Some historians have criticized President Roosevelt for being too forceful and not doing enough to help minorities gain equal rights. For the most part, though, TR was considered to have been a bold leader who was just right for the times. Teddy Roosevelt died peacefully in his sleep on January 6, 1919.